JANICE VANCLEAVE'S
FIRST-PLACE SCIENCE FAIR PROJECTS™

STEP-BY-STEP
SCIENCE EXPERIMENTS IN

ENERGY

rosen publishing's
rosen central

NEW YORK

This edition first published in 2013 by:

The Rosen Publishing Group, Inc.
29 East 21st Street
New York, NY 10010

Additional content and end matter copyright © 2013 by The Rosen Publishing
Group, Inc.

Library of Congress Cataloging-in-Publication Data

VanCleave, Janice Pratt.
Step-by-step science experiments in energy/Janice VanCleave.
    p. cm. — (Janice VanCleave's first-place science fair projects)
Includes bibliographical references and index.
ISBN 978-1-4488-6979-4 (lib. bdg.) —
ISBN 978-1-4488-8471-1 (pbk.) —
ISBN 978-1-4488-8472-8 (6-pack)
1. Force and energy—Experiments—Juvenile literature. 2. Science projects—
Juvenile literature. I. Title.
QC73.4.V364 2013
531'.6078—dc23

                                                                2012006835

Manufactured in the United States of America

CPSIA Compliance Information: Batch #S12YA: For further information, contact Rosen Publishing, New York, New York, at 1-800-237-9932.

This edition published by arrangement with and permission of John Wiley & Sons,
Inc., Hoboken, New Jersey.

Originally published as *Energy For Every Kid.* Copyright © 2006 by Janice
VanCleave

CONTENTS

Do you like roller coasters? Have you ever wondered what makes a roller coaster climb to the top of the first hill and race down the other side? The answer is energy. Energy is the ability to make change and do work. We use energy every day to do many things, not only to move roller coasters. We use energy to ride a bike and power a car. We use energy to heat our homes and cook dinner. There are many ways to produce energy, such as using your muscles or starting a fire. We can use up a source of energy, or we can store energy to use at a later time. Some sources of energy will last forever. Even gravity can be a source of energy.

There are many different kinds of energy. The most basic form is mechanical energy. There are two kinds of mechanical energy. Potential, or stored, energy is the energy an object has because of its position. A yo-yo with its string wound up has potential energy. Water held back by a dam has potential energy. These both have stored energy that can be set free under the right conditions. Kinetic is the energy an object has because of its motion. Gravity is a source of kinetic energy when it makes things fall to Earth. The more mass and speed an object has, the greater its kinetic energy is. A car traveling 55 miles per hour (89 kmh) has more kinetic energy than a baseball traveling at the same speed because it's heavier. However, a thrown baseball has greater kinetic energy than a car at rest.

Energy is often thought of as the ability to do work. Mechanical energy has the ability to move an object by applying force to it. A raised hammer, for example, has potential energy. This means that it has stored energy and is ready to do work. When the hammer is swung toward a nail in a block of wood, the potential energy changes into kinetic energy. The kinetic energy allows the hammer to apply force to the nail. The force displaces, or moves, the nail and drives it into the wood. The hammer regains potential energy after it has been raised for another swing. Energy can't be created or destroyed. It can, however, change forms. All forms of energy can be sorted as kinetic or potential.

Light is called electromagnetic (EM) energy because it's made up of waves of electricity and waves of magnetic force. Other forms of EM energy include X-rays and radio waves. Light is the only form of EM energy that we can see without special instruments. EM energy is kinetic energy. It never stops moving once it's produced, as long as nothing gets in its way.

Light is the energy that allows us to see the world around us. It's made up of different length waves that create all the colors we see. When light hits an object, some of the waves are reflected and some are absorbed. We see the waves that are reflected. When light hits grass, for example, the grass absorbs all the wavelengths of the colors except green. Green light waves are reflected. That's why grass looks green.

Did you know that sound is a form of kinetic energy? Sound, like light, travels in waves. Sound waves can travel through all kinds of matter, including solids, liquids, and gases. The matter through which sound waves travel is called the medium. Sound can't travel when there is no medium. For example, sound can't travel in outer space because there's no matter. Sound waves cause matter to vibrate, or move up and down and back and forth very quickly. This allows the sound wave to travel through the medium. Changes to the height and length of sound waves cause different sounds. Some sounds are too high for people to hear, and some are too low.

Chemical energy is potential energy stored in the bonds that hold atoms and molecules together. When these bonds break, the chemical energy can move to another molecule or atom, or it can be released in another form. For example, burning coal or oil breaks the bonds between their molecules and releases energy in the form of light and heat.

Nuclear energy is another type of potential energy. It's the energy that holds an atom's nucleus, or center, together. It can be released by breaking the nucleus of an atom apart. Nuclear energy can also be released by combining the centers of atoms. This is how the sun makes heat and light.

How to Use This Book

The experiments in this book were selected for their ability to explain concepts in basic terms with little complexity. One of the main objectives of the book is to present the fun of learning about energy through experiments.

Read each chapter slowly and follow procedures carefully. You will learn best if each section is read in order, as there is some buildup of information as the book progresses. Follow these general instructions when conducting the experiments:

1. Read each activity completely before starting.
2. Collect the needed supplies. You will have less frustration and more fun if all the necessary materials for the activities are ready before you start. You lose your train of thought when you have to stop and search for supplies.
3. Do not rush through the activity. Follow each step very carefully; never skip steps, and do not add your own. Safety is of utmost importance, and by reading each activity before starting, then following the instructions exactly, you can feel confident that no unexpected results will occur.
4. Observe. If your results are not the same as described in the activity, carefully reread the instructions and start over from step 1.

This is an introductory book about energy that is designed to teach facts and problem-solving strategies. Each experiment introduces concepts about energy in a way that makes learning useful and fun. So let's get started!

1 UPHILL

PURPOSE: To compare the work done in moving an object by different methods.

MATERIALS:

- scissors
- rubber band
- paper clip
- paper hole punch
- 4-by-10-inch (10-by-25-cm) piece of corrugated cardboard
- metric ruler
- pen
- 4 tablespoons (60 ml) of dirt (sand or salt will work)
- empty soda can with metal tab
- 24-inch (60-cm) piece of string
- 4 or more books

PROCEDURE:

1. Cut the rubber band to form one long piece.
2. Tie one end of the rubber band to the paper clip. Open one end of the paper clip to form a hook.
3. Using the paper hole punch, cut a hole in the center of the edge of the cardboard.
4. Tie the free end of the rubber band in the hole in the cardboard. The top of the paper clip should reach the center of the cardboard.
5. Use the ruler and pen to draw a line across the cardboard, making it even with the top of the paper clip. Label the line 0.

6. Then draw as many lines as possible .39 inch (1 cm) apart below the 0 line. You have made a scale.

7. Pour the dirt into the soda can.
8. Thread the string through the hole in the tab of the soda can. Tie the ends of the string together to make a loop.
9. Place the string loop over the hook on the scale.
10. Stack all of the books except one. Lean the extra book against the stacked books to form a ramp as shown.

11. Stand the can next to the stack of books. Then lift the can straight up by pulling on the top of the cardboard until the bottom of the can is even with the top of the books. Note the scale line closest to the top of the paper clip hook.

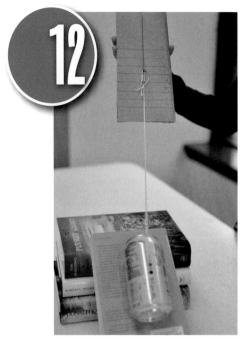

12. Lay the can on the book ramp. With the scale still attached to the string, drag the can to the top of the ramp. Again note the scale line closest to the top of the paper clip hook as the can is being moved.

RESULTS The rubber band stretches more when the can is lifted straight up than when it is pulled up the ramp. So the number on the scale when you pulled the can straight up was higher than the number when you were pulling the can up the ramp.

WHY? Gravity pulls the can down. When you lift the can straight up, the rubber band scale indicates the full pull of gravity, which is the weight of the can. The work done in lifting the can to the height of the stacked books is the product of the weight of the can times the height of the books.

A ramp is a tilted surface used to move objects to a higher level. A ramp is called a machine because it is a device that helps you do work. When using a machine, you generally have to use less effort. For example, the decrease in the amount the can on the ramp stretched the rubber band indicates that the force needed to pull the can up the ramp is less than that needed to lift the can straight up. It takes less effort to drag the can up the ramp, but the can needs to be moved a longer distance.

EQUAL

PURPOSE: To demonstrate conservation of mass during a chemical reaction.

- two 3-ounce (90-ml) paper cups
- measuring spoons
- tap water
- 1 tablespoon (5 ml) Epsom salts
- spoon
- liquid school glue
- food scale
- paper towel

PROCEDURE:

1. In one of the paper cups, add 2 tablespoons (10 ml) of water and the Epsom salts. Stir the mixture until very little or no Epsom salts are left at the bottom of the cup.

2. Pour 1 tablespoon (5 ml) of liquid school glue into the second cup.

3. Set both cups on the scale. Note the appearance of the contents of each cup and their combined weight.

4. Pour the Epsom salts and water mixture into the cup of glue. Stir the contents of the cup. Note the appearance of the mixture in the cup.

5. With both the empty cup and the cup with the mixture on the scale, again note their combined weight and compare it to the combined weight of the cups before mixing their contents.

6. Once the weights have been compared, scoop out the white solid blob that has formed in the cup and place it on the paper towel. Fold the towel around the blob and squeeze the towel to press the extra liquid out of the blob. How does the blob differ from the reactants from which it was formed?

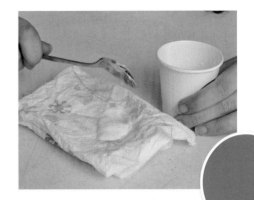

RESULTS Originally, one cup contains a clear liquid made of Epsom salts and water, and the other contains white liquid glue. After mixing, a white solid blob of material is formed with some of the liquid left. The weights of the cups and their contents are the same before and after mixing.

WHY? The mixture of Epsom salts and water forms a solution (a mixture of a substance that has been dissolved in a liquid). The liquid glue is also a solution containing different substances dissolved in water. When these two solutions are combined, a chemical reaction occurs between the materials as indicated by the formation of a white solid material. Even though the reactants break apart and recombine in different ways, all the original parts are contained inside the cup. Thus, when you weigh the cups the second time, there is no change in weight, which indicates there is no change in mass. So the conservation of mass during a chemical reaction is demonstrated.

HOPPER

PURPOSE: To demonstrate the relationship between kinetic and potential energy.

MATERIALS:

- 8-by-8-inch (20-by-20-cm) sheet of paper (use green paper if available)
- ruler
- pencil

PROCEDURE:

1. Fold the paper in half from side to side twice.
2. Unfold one of the folds.
3. Fold the top corners A and B over as shown.
4. Unfold the corners. Use the ruler and pencil to draw lines C and D across the paper.

5. Fold the paper along line C. Then unfold the paper. Repeat folding and unfolding along line D.

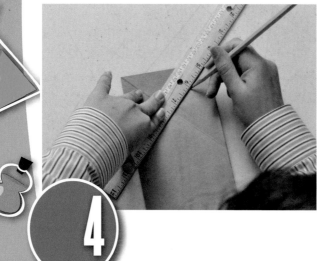

6. Push in the sides of the top of the paper along the folded lines. Press the top down to form a triangle.
7. Fold the bottom of the paper over to meet the edge of the triangle at the top.
8. Bend one of the triangle points along the fold line. Then fold the side of the paper over to meet the center fold line.
9. Repeat step 8 with the other triangle point.

10. Fold the bottom edge over. Then fold part of it down as shown. You have made a leaping frog.
11. Use the pencil to draw eyes on the frog.

12. Stand the frog on a table and push down on its back with your finger so that the frog's back legs are compressed. Then quickly run your finger down the frog's back and off the end.

RESULTS The frog will leap forward and possibly turn a somersault.

WHY? When you press down on the frog, you are doing work on the frog, causing its folded legs to compress together much like a spring would be compressed. In this condition, the frog has potential energy. When you run your finger down the frog's back and off the folded end, this end is more compressed and the frog's head is raised. When you release the frog, the potential energy is transferred to kinetic energy as the frog leaps forward.

HIGHER

PURPOSE: To determine the effect that height has on the gravitational potential energy of an object.

MATERIALS:
- 2 cups (500 ml) dry rice
- sock
- bathroom scale

PROCEDURE:
1. Pour the rice in the sock and tie a knot in the sock.

17

2. Place the scale on the floor.

3. Hold the sock just above the scale.

4. Drop the sock on the scale and note how much the weight changes.

5. Repeat step 4, holding the sock about waist high above the scale.

RESULTS The weight on the scale changes more when the sock is dropped from a higher position.

WHY? The gravitational potential energy of an object is equal to the work done to raise the object, and assuming no friction with air as it falls, the gravitational potential energy is equal to the work the object can do when it drops from its raised position. The work done to raise the sock is equal to the force weight of the sock times its height above the scale. As the height increases, more work is done to raise the sock, so the gravitational potential energy of the sock increases. This is demonstrated by the change in the reading on the scale. The weight changed more when the scale was struck by the sock dropped from a higher position because more work was done on the scale by this sock than by the sock dropped from a lower height.

SWINGER

PURPOSE: To demonstrate the effect of velocity on kinetic energy.

MATERIALS:

- 1 cup dry rice
- sock
- 3-foot (0.9-m) piece of string
- sheet of copy paper
- transparent tape
- unopened can of food
- pencil

PROCEDURE:

1. Pour the rice in the sock and tie a knot in the sock.

2. Tie one end of the string around the knot in the sock.

3. Tape the free end of the string to the top edge of a table. Adjust the length of the string by pulling on it so that the sock hangs about 1 inch (2.5 cm) above the floor. Then place one or more pieces of tape over the string to hold it in place.

4. Tape the paper to the floor underneath the sock so that the sock hangs above the edge of the paper.

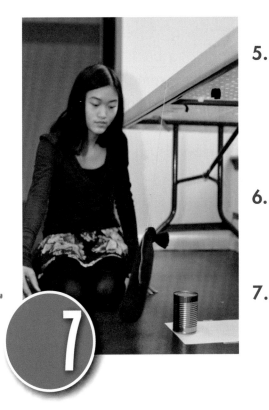

5. Set the can of food on the edge of the paper so that its side touches the sock.

6. Pull the sock away from the can.

7. Release the sock and allow it to hit the can.

8. With the pencil, mark on the paper how much the can moved.

9. Repeat steps 6 through 8 two or more times, but pull the sock farther away from the can each time.

RESULTS The farther the sock is pulled away from the can of food, the farther the can is moved.

WHY? The hanging sock is an example of a pendulum, which is a suspended weight that is free to swing back and forth. The weight and therefore the mass of the sock remained the same. The change was in the height of the sock. As the height of the sock increased, the velocity of the sock increased. Since the kinetic energy of the swinging sock depends on the sock's mass and its velocity, the kinetic energy increases as the height of the sock increases. This was shown by an increase in the distance the can moved when hit by the swinging sock. With more kinetic energy, the sock does more work on the can, thus moving it a farther distance.

MAGIC CAN

PURPOSE: To demonstrate how friction affects the change between mechanical potential and mechanical kinetic energy.

MATERIALS:

- 2 plastic coffee can lids
- 13-ounce (368-g) coffee can, empty, with top and bottom removed by an adult
- pencil
- 3- to 4-inch (7.5- to 10-cm)-long rubber band
- 2 paper clips
- 10 pennies
- masking tape

PROCEDURE:

1. Hold the lid in your hand.

2. Use the pencil to make a hole in the center of each lid. The holes should be large enough for the rubber band to go through.

3. Thread one end of the rubber band through each hole from the inside of the lids.

4. Clip one of the paper clips to each end of the rubber band to keep it from pulling back through the lid. Pull on the rubber band to pull the paper clips snugly against the lids.

5. With the insides of the lids facing each other, stack the coins and wrap tape around them. Use tape to secure the stack of coins to the middle of one strand of the rubber band.

6. Slightly fold one of the lids and push it inside the can.

7. Snap the other lid over one end of the can, then pull the lid inside the can out and snap it in place at the other end. Note: If the coins touch the side of the can, tighten the rubber band by pulling its ends through one lid and tying a knot in them. Adjust the coins so that they stay in the center.

8. Place the can on its side on the floor and push the can so that it rolls forward. Observe the motion of the can until it stops moving. Note: The can needs about 10 feet (3 m) or more for rolling.

RESULTS The can rolls forward and stops, then rolls backward and stops again. Some cans roll back and forth several times.

WHY? You do work on the can by pushing it. This work gives the can mechanical kinetic energy, so it rolls across the floor. As the can rolls, the rubber band winds up, storing more and more potential energy. This energy is called elastic potential energy, which is a form of mechanical potential energy. When the can stops, the rubber band starts to unwind, and the elastic potential energy stored in it is changed to mechanical kinetic energy, causing the can to roll backward. The can continues to roll after the rubber band is unwound due to inertia (the tendency of an object in motion to continue to move forward), causing the rubber band to wind up again. This winding and unwinding of the rubber band can continue several times until all the mechanical kinetic energy is transferred into other types of energy, mostly heat from friction. Then the can stops.

STANDING

PURPOSE: To determine how the frequency of a vibrating source affects the standing waves produced.

MATERIALS:

- paper towel
- transparent tape
- 12-inch (30-cm) piece of string
- Slinky

PROCEDURE:

1. Fold the paper towel in half three times and wrap it around the bottom of a chair leg. Secure the paper towel by wrapping a piece of tape around it. The paper towel is used to protect the surface of the chair leg.

1

2. Stretch the Slinky out on the floor to a length of about 6 to 8 feet (1.8 to 2.4 m). Use the string to tie one end of the slinky to the chair leg over the paper towel.

3. Holding the free end of the Slinky, quickly move the end from side to side one time to send a wave down the spring. Observe the motion of the wave.

4. Slowly move the end of the Slinky from side to side, changing the number of side-to-side motions until standing waves are formed. Try to move the end the same distance each time.

5. Repeat step 4, but quickly move the end of the Slinky from side to side.

RESULTS As the speed of the side-to-side motion of the end of the Slinky increases, the number of standing waves increases.

WHY? A wave that does not appear to be moving is a standing wave. Points on the wave called nodes stay in place while areas between the nodes move back and forth, alternately forming crests and troughs called antinodes with each motion. In this experiment, standing waves were formed by vibrating the end of a Slinky. The frequency of vibration increased as the speed of the side-to-side motion increased. As the frequency of the vibrating source (the end of the Slinky) increased, the number of standing waves increased.

ASTRO SOUNDS

PURPOSE: To determine how amplitudes affect the loudness of sound.

MATERIALS:

- metal Slinky
- 16-ounce (480-ml) plastic cup

PROCEDURE:

1. Stick one end of the Slinky into the bottom of the cup.

2. Stand with the open end of the cup over one ear and the Slinky stretched so that its free end rests on the floor. Lean slightly so that the Slinky is as straight as possible and not touching your body.

3. With your hand, squeeze three or four coils of the Slinky together near the bottom of the cup, then release the coils. Note the loudness of the sound produced.

4. Repeat step 3, but compress eight or more coils together.

RESULTS A louder sound is heard when more coils are compressed together.

WHY? The sound bounces back and forth as the waves move through the springs of the Slinky and reflect off the bottom of the cup and the floor. When you compress more coils together, you hear a louder sound because you have put more energy into the sound. Loudness is related to the amount of energy carried by a wave. The amplitude of a wave is an indication of its energy; the greater the energy, the greater the amplitude. For sound waves, this means the compressions are more crowded and the rarefactions are more spread out. The greater the amplitude of a sound, the louder the sound.

A scale of sound intensities (sound wave energy per second) has been developed with an intensity unit of decibels (dB). A decibel of 0 is a sound so soft, it can barely be heard. Whispering is about 10 dB, normal conversation is 60 to 70 dB, loud music is about 90 to 100 dB, a jet engine is about 100 dB, and pain is caused by a sound intensity greater than about 120 dB.

BRIGHTER

PURPOSE: To show that excited electrons give off light when they lose energy.

MATERIALS:

- scissors
- newsprint
- white index card
- transparent tape
- fluorescent yellow highlighter pen
- incandescent lamp

PROCEDURE:

1. Cut a piece of newsprint slightly smaller than the index card.
2. Secure the newsprint to the card with tape.

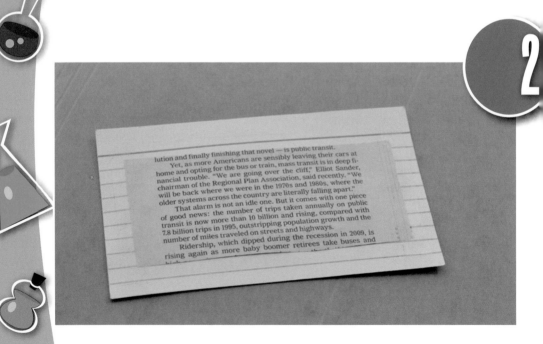

3. Use the pen to highlight part of the print on the card.

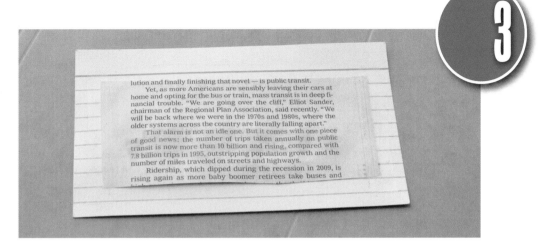

4. Hold the card so that the light from the incandescent lamp shines on it. Make note of the brightness of the highlighted areas on the card.

5. Repeat step 4 using sunlight.

RESULTS The highlighted area is brighter when viewed in sunlight.

WHY? Fluorescent ink has a special chemical that absorbs invisible ultraviolet radiation and changes it to visible light that is the same color as the ink. This happens because electrons in the chemical absorb ultraviolet radiation, causing some of the electrons in the chemical to be excited. The excited electrons lose their excess energy in the form of photons of visible light. Thus, the ink is absorbing invisible radiation and emitting visible light of the same color as the ink.

For yellow fluorescent ink, yellow photons are emitted. Yellow fluorescent ink has yellow pigment that reflects yellow photons from visible light striking it, plus the special chemical that absorbs UV radiation and emits yellow light. With this combined yellow light, the ink is extra bright in color. If the ink is viewed in visible light only, such as light produced by an incandescent lamp, the ink looks yellow because of the reflected yellow light, but it is not an extra bright yellow. Also, some incandescent light gives off a slightly yellow color, making the card appear yellowish. Thus, the area highlighted with the yellow ink may blend in with the yellowed paper, making it difficult to see.

LIGHT PAINTING

PURPOSE: To demonstrate reflection of light.

MATERIALS:

- sheet of white copy paper
- flashlight
- 2 pieces of construction paper—1 yellow, 1 red

PROCEDURE:

1. Fold the white paper in half from top to bottom.

2. Stand the paper on a table. This will be your screen.

3. In a darkened room, turn on the flashlight and shine it on the white screen. Note the color of the screen.

4. Lay the flashlight on the table beside the screen as shown.

5. Hold the sheet of yellow paper about 12 inches (30 cm) or more in front of the white paper. Then slowly move the yellow paper toward the screen until it is as close as the bulb end of the flashlight. As you move the yellow paper, note the color of the screen.

6. Repeat step 5 using the sheet of red paper.

RESULTS The screen looks white when the light is directed toward it but looks yellow when the light first hits the yellow paper and red when the light first hits the red paper.

WHY? The yellow and red paper are colored because of pigments (natural substances that give color to a material). The light from the flashlight is basically white, so it has the rainbow colors (red, orange, yellow, green, blue, indigo, and violet). When white light hits a white object, such as the paper, the material absorbs very little light and reflects all the colored light. All the reflected colored light blended together produces white light, so the object looks white. The color you see depends on the colors reflected by the object that reach your eye. The pigments in the yellow paper absorb all the colors in white light except yellow. It reflects yellow light toward the screen, which reflects it to your eye. Thus, the screen appears to be yellow. The same is true for the red paper: it absorbs all the colors in white light except red, which it reflects.

11 LOSER

PURPOSE: To demonstrate heat transfer by conduction.

MATERIALS:
- metal cookie sheet
- 18-inch (45-cm) piece of string

PROCEDURE:

1. Press your right hand against the surface and near one end of the cookie sheet. Using your other hand, stretch the string around the hand that is on the cookie sheet to outline it.

1

2. With the string in place, continue to press your hand against the cookie sheet for thirty or more seconds. Measure the time in seconds by counting one thousand and one, one thousand and two, one thou- sand and three, and so on, to one thousand and thirty.

3. Before lifting your hand from the cookie sheet, place the fingers on your left hand against its surface at the oppo- site end. Note how warm or cool the cookie sheet feels.

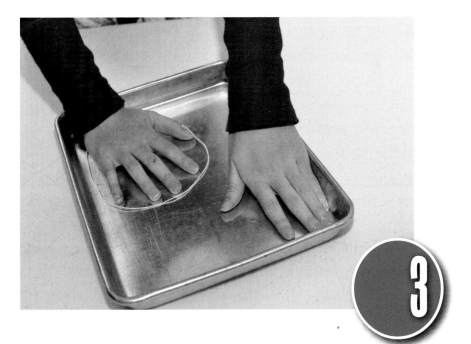

4

4. Lift your right hand and touch your left hand to the area of the cookie sheet within the string outline that was covered by your right hand. Note how warm or cool the area feels.

RESULTS The cookie sheet feels warmer in the area within the string outline.

WHY? Conduction is the process by which heat is transferred between objects in contact with each other. The heat moves from the warmer object to the cooler one. The cookie sheet is at room temperature and your body temperature is about 98.6°F (37°C), which is generally much warmer than room temperature. When you touch your hand to the cookie sheet, heat from your hand moves to the cookie sheet because of conduction. The thermal energy of the skin touching the cookie sheet decreases, and the thermal energy of the cookie sheet increases. Thus, the cookie sheet's temperature within the string outline increases. Outside the string, the temperature of the cookie sheet does not increase, so it feels cooler. The sensation of coolness or warmness depends on how much heat leaves or enters your skin. The more heat leaving the skin, the cooler the object feels.

STREAMERS

PURPOSE: To demonstrate convection currents due to temperature differences.

MATERIALS:

- masking tape
- pen
- four 9-ounce (270-ml) transparent plastic cups
- warm and cold tap water
- 2 ice cubes
- drinking straw
- red food coloring
- adult helper

PROCEDURE:

1. Use the tape and pen to label two cups "Cold" and the two remaining cups "Warm."

2. Fill one of the cold cups three-fourths full with cold tap water. Add the ice to this cup.
3. Stir the icy water several times with the straw. Remove and discard the ice, then pour about half of the water into the other cold cup.

41

4. Add ten drops of red food coloring to one of the cups of cold water. Stir with the straw.
5. Ask an adult to fill the warm cups half full with warm tap water. Add ten drops of food coloring to one of the cups of warm water. Stir with the straw.
6. Set the cup of uncolored warm water on a table and sit so that you are eye level with the cup.

7. Stand the straw in the colored cold water. Keep the water in the straw by placing your finger over the open end.

8. Place the straw in the cup of uncolored warm water. Slightly raise your finger from the end of the straw to allow the colored cold water to leave the straw. Observe the movement of the colored water.

9. Remove the straw from the water and observe the contents of the cup periodically for about five minutes.
10. Repeat steps 6 through 9, but use uncolored cold water in step 6 and colored warm water in step 7.

RESULTS The colored cold water flows out of the straw and settles on the bottom of the cup of warm water. The colored warm water flows out of the straw and rises to the surface of the cold water. The colored warm water mixes with the cold water as it rises, thus coloring the cold water. But a darker layer of colored water forms on the surface of the cold water.

WHY? Convection is the transfer of heat by moving fluid, such as water, due to differences in temperature. Warm-water molecules have more energy and move around faster than less energetic cold-water molecules. The speedy warm-water molecules tend to move away from each other. So warm water, with its molecules spaced farther apart, is less dense than cold water. When the colored cold water was released at the bottom of a cup filled with warm water, the denser cold water sank to the bottom of the cup. When the colored warm water was released at the bottom of the cup filled with cold water, the warm water, which was less dense than the cold water, rose to the surface. During its movement to the surface, there was some mixing of the colored warm water with the uncolored cold water. But most of it rose to the surface, forming a dark layer there. In the cup as in nature, cold surface water sinks as the warmer water rises and takes its place. This rising of warm water and sinking of cold water produces convection currents.

STRAIGHT THROUGH

PURPOSE: To compare the effect of materials on the transfer of infrared radiation.

MATERIALS:

- 6-by-6-inch (15-by-15-cm) piece of white plastic garbage bag

- 6-by-6-inch (15-by-15-cm) piece of white poster board
- desk lamp

PROCEDURE:

1. Turn the lamp on and adjust it so that the light shines down.

2. Hold one hand, palm side up, about 4 inches (10 cm) below the bulb of the lamp for five seconds. Measure the time in seconds by counting one thousand and one, one thousand and two, and so on. Note how warm or cool your hand feels while under the light. Caution: Do not hold your hand closer than 4 inches (10 cm) below the bulb. Remove your hand if your skin starts to feel uncomfortably warm.

3. Remove your hand from under the light and allow it to cool for five seconds. Then cover your palm with the square of white plastic and repeat step 2.

4. Repeat step 2, but cover your hand with the square of white poster board.

RESULTS The skin of your hand feels warmest without a covering, medium warm with the plastic covering, and coolest with the poster board covering.

WHY? The lamp gives off infrared radiation, which is absorbed by your skin, causing your skin to feel warm. The poster board blocks infrared radiation; the plastic only blocks some of it. This is why your hand feels warmest with no covering, medium warm when covered with the plastic, and coolest when covered with the poster board.

SEPARATOR

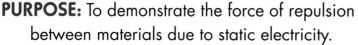

PURPOSE: To demonstrate the force of repulsion between materials due to static electricity.

MATERIALS:

* transparent tape

PROCEDURE:

1. Tear off a strip of tape about 8 inches (20 cm) long from the roll of tape.
2. Stick one end of the strip of tape to the edge of a table so that most of the tape hangs down from the table's edge.

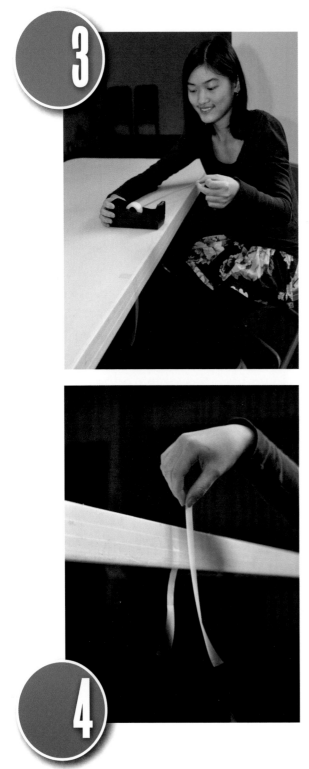

3. Tear off a second 8-inch (20 cm) piece of tape from the tape roll.

4. Hold one edge of the second strip of tape near but not touching the tape hanging from the table. Observe the immediate position of the two hanging strips of tape.

RESULTS The pieces of tape immediately move apart when placed near one another.

WHY? When you pull the tape off the roll, you are pulling some atoms in the tape apart, which is an example of charging by friction. As the sticky and unsticky sides of the tape separate, electrons are either lost or gained by the strip. Assume the strip gains electrons and is negatively charged. There is a buildup of negative charges on the tape. Since the two strips have like charges and like charges repel one another, the strips move apart. The repulsion of the strips is caused by static electricity. In time the static charge is lost. Static discharge is the loss of static electricity. It occurs when electrons on the strips of tape are picked up by air molecules or more likely water molecules in the air that transfer the electrons to other materials they touch, and so on. Water molecules are polarized (have a positive end and a negative end). The positive end attracts and holds the electrons to carry them off. This explains why there is little static electricity when the humidity (measure of the amount of water vapor in air) is high.

The static discharge from the tape strips was slow and quiet, but sometimes static discharge is very rapid and noisy, such as lightning (visible static discharge between clouds or a cloud and Earth) accompanied by thunder (loud sound produced by the expansion of air that has been heated by lightning).

ATTRACTIVE

PURPOSE: To demonstrate static electricity.

MATERIALS:

- sheet of copy paper
- salt shaker with salt
- 9-inch (22.5-cm) round balloon
- wool scarf

PROCEDURE:

1. Lay the paper on a table.

2. Sprinkle a thin layer of salt over the center of the paper.

3. Inflate and tie the balloon.

4. Charge the balloon by rubbing it back and forth on the scarf five or more times.

5. Hold the balloon near but not touching the salt.

RESULTS The particles of salt jump up and stick to the balloon.

WHY? Rubbing the balloon on the scarf results in electrons moving from the scarf to the balloon. When the rubbing stops and the balloon and scarf are separated, the electric charges stop moving. The electric charges on each material remain stationary, so each has a static charge. The balloon has a negative charge. When you hold it near the salt particles, it causes the salt to be polarized by electrostatic induction. The salt still has a balance of positive and negative charges, but these charges have separated because of the charged balloon. The electrons on the side of the salt facing the negatively charged balloon are repelled, leaving a buildup of positive charges on that side. The attraction between this positive surface and the negatively charged balloon is great enough to lift the salt and stick it to the balloon.

STRONGER

PURPOSE: To demonstrate the effect of magnetic potential energy.

MATERIALS:

- 12-inch (30-cm) piece of string
- paper clip
- transparent tape

- 5 or more books
- bar magnet
- scissors

PROCEDURE:

1. Tie the string to the paper clip.
2. Tape the free end of the string to a table.

3. With your hand, hold the paper clip and raise it up above the table until the string is taut.

4. Release the paper clip and observe its motion.

5. Stack the books on the table. Place the magnet so that one end extends over the edge of the top book. Position the books and magnet so that the magnet is over the paper clip.

6. Touch the end of the paper clip under the end of the magnet, then slowly pull the end of the string until the paper clip is suspended in the air and only slightly separated from the magnet.

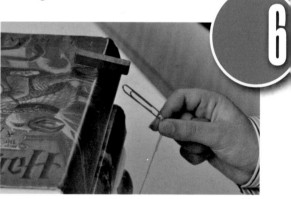

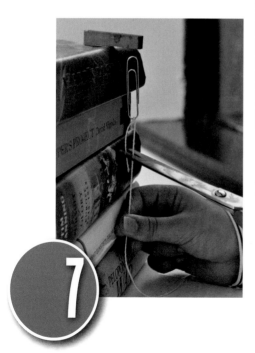

7. With the paper clip suspended and separated from the magnet, cut the string and observe the motion of the paper clip.

RESULTS Without the magnet, the raised paper clip falls down toward the table when it is released. When the paper clip is suspended but separated from the magnet and the string is cut, the paper clip moves up toward the magnet.

WHY? When the paper clip is raised with your hand, it has gravitational potential energy because of its position in Earth's gravitational force field. If the table is the reference point, then the gravitational potential energy (stored energy) depends on how high above the table the paper clip is raised. When an object with gravitational potential energy is free to move, the force of gravity acting upon it causes it to move toward the center of Earth. So when you released the paper clip, it moved in a direction that reduced its potential energy. This direction was down toward the table. The paper clip's gravitational potential energy was transformed into kinetic energy (energy of motion). Note that the paper clip moves in the direction of the force acting on it.

When the paper clip is held in a raised position above the table by the magnetic force of the magnet, it has two kinds of potential energy. One is gravitational potential energy due to being raised above the table. The other is magnetic potential energy due to the paper clip's position in the magnetic force field around the magnet. Since the magnetic force is toward the magnet, the two forces acting on the paper clip are in opposite directions. When the string was cut, the paper clip moved upward toward the magnet, which was the direction of the greater force. This motion caused the paper clip's magnetic potential energy to be decreased and its gravitational potential energy to be increased.

17 COOLER

PURPOSE: To demonstrate an endothermic reaction.

MATERIALS:

- ½ cup (125 ml) vinegar
- 1-quart (1 L) jar
- thermometer

- 2 tablespoons (30 ml) baking soda

PROCEDURE:

1. Pour the vinegar into the jar.

1

2. Stand the thermometer in the jar.

3. After two or more minutes, note the reading on the thermometer.

4. With the thermometer in the jar, add the baking soda.

5. Observe the thermometer and note whether the reading on the thermometer increased or decreased.

RESULTS The temperature of the mixture decreases.

WHY? Before adding the vinegar and baking soda together, they are about room temperature. When the vinegar and baking soda are mixed together, a chemical reaction occurs, resulting in products that include a gas. The foaming action indicates gas production. The temperature of the mixture decreases, which indicates that heat energy is taken out of the mixture. Thus, the reaction is an endothermic reaction in which energy is taken in and stored as potential energy in chemical bonds.

HALF TIME

PURPOSE: To model radioactive decay.

MATERIALS:
- large bowl
- scissors
- sheet of copy paper

PROCEDURE:
1. Set the bowl on a table.
2. Count out five seconds by counting one thousand one, one thousand two, and so on, as you cut the paper in half. You need to estimate the line across the paper that divides it in half.

59

3. Place one of the paper halves in the bowl. Keep the other paper half and repeat step 2.

4. Continue to repeat steps 2 and 3 six times, or until the paper is too small to safely cut it.

5. To determine the number of half-lives represented, count the number of paper pieces in the bowl.

RESULTS The paper is divided seven or more times.

WHY? The time it takes for half of a radioactive element to change to another stable element is called its half-life. The half-life in this activity is five seconds. At the end of five seconds, half of the paper was placed in the bowl to demonstrate the change that half of the radioactive material had decayed to a stable material. After another five seconds, half of the remaining sheet was placed in the bowl. As time passed, the amount of material in the bowl increased and the amount out of the bowl decreased, just as all radioactive elements will eventually decrease. While the half-life in this activity was five seconds, the half-lives of some radioactive elements are much shorter, whereas others are hours, days, years, or even billions of years.

19 COLLECTORS

PURPOSE: To demonstrate how natural gas rises.

MATERIALS:

- ¼ cup (63 ml) tap water
- ½-pint (250-ml) plastic bottle, such as a water bottle
- ¼ cup (63 ml) cooking oil
- 1 effervescent tablet, such as Alka-Seltzer
- 9-inch (22.5-cm) round balloon

PROCEDURE:

1. Pour the water into the bottle.

2. Pour the oil into the bottle.

3. Break the effervescent tablet in half and drop the two pieces into the bottle. Immediately stretch the mouth of the balloon over the opening in the bottle.

4. Observe the contents of the bottle and the balloon.

RESULTS A gas produced in the water moved upward through the oil. The gas partially inflated the balloon.

WHY? Oil and natural gas formed from prehistoric organisms that lived in the ocean millions of years ago. The parts of these organisms that collected on the ocean floor were slowly buried and compressed under layers of sediment. Heat and pressure changed the sediment (rock particle transported and deposited by water, wind, or glaciers) into rock and the remains of the organisms into oil and natural gas.

In areas with porous (having holes) rock, the oil and gas slowly filled the tiny holes in the rock. This porous rock was called reservoir rock by geologists (scientists who study Earth) because oil and natural gas collected and were stored in it. Because the holes in the reservoir rock were usually filled with water, the less dense oil and gas, which are not soluble in water, moved upward through the water in the rock. When the oil and gas reached a nonporous (without holes) rock, such as shale, the oil and gas collected below it. Natural gas is usually found in pools above oil because it is less dense than oil, as you can see from this experiment. Enough gas collected above the oil in this experiment to partially inflate the balloon.

ALL ALONE

PURPOSE: To demonstrate that plants can recycle material needed for food and energy.

MATERIALS:

- ½ cup (125 ml) small gravel
- 1-quart (1-L) large-mouthed plastic jar with lid
- 1 cup (250 ml) potting soil
- iced-tea spoon

- small plant that will fit inside the jar, such as very small fern, miniature African violet, ivy
- ½ cup (125 ml) tap water
- paper towel

PROCEDURE:

1. Pour the gravel into the jar. Shake the jar gently to evenly spread the gravel.

2. Pour the soil into the jar and again shake to evenly spread the soil.

3. Use the spoon to dig a hole in the soil equal to the size of the plant's roots.

4. Set the plant in the hole in the soil. With the spoon, cover the plant's roots with soil and press the soil firmly around the plant. Take care not to damage the plant's roots.

5. Pour the water on the plant.

6. Use the paper towel to clean the inside surface of the jar above the soil.
7. Seal the jar with the lid.
8. Set the jar in a lighted area but out of direct sunlight.
9. Observe the contents of the jar periodically for two days. If the inside of the jar is continuously covered with water, open the jar, dry the water with a paper towel, and close the jar again.
10. Observe the contents of the jar periodically for four or more weeks.

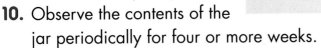

RESULTS The inside of the jar appears cloudy at times and the plant grows.

WHY? Potted plants can live in a closed container for a time as long as they have access to light. This is because plants are autotrophs (organisms that can make their own food). Plants recycle materials needed for food and energy production. During photosynthesis in plants, carbon dioxide and water are changed to glucose, oxygen, and water. During respiration, the glucose, oxygen, and water are changed back to carbon dioxide and water plus energy. Plants do need access to light, however, because light energy cannot be recycled.

TOP TO BOTTOM

PURPOSE: To model an energy pyramid in an ecosystem.

MATERIALS:

- sheet of copy paper
- scissors
- pen
- ruler
- transparent tape

PROCEDURE:

1. Fold the paper with its top edge against an adjacent side. Crease the fold by pressing it flat with your fingers. Cut off the bottom strip from the paper and discard.

2. Unfold the paper and refold it diagonally the opposite way. Crease the fold as before.

3. Open the paper. Using the pen and the ruler, divide three of the four triangles made by the fold lines into four sections as shown.

4. In section A, write the levels of a food chain as shown: producer, 1st-order consumer, 2nd-order consumer, 3rd-order consumer. In sections B and C, give examples of the different levels of a food chain. You may wish to add drawings or pictures cut from magazines.

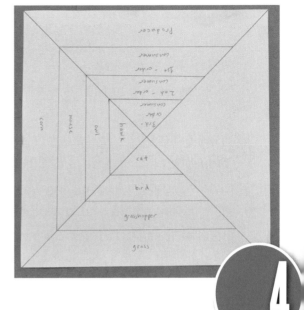

5. Cut along the fold line separating sections A and D to the center of the paper.

6. Overlap section D with section A. Secure them together with tape. Stand the paper structure on its open base and you have a pyramid.

RESULTS You have made a model of the pyramid of energy in an ecosystem.

WHY? Plants produce food, which is chemical potential energy. Only about 10 percent of the food energy produced by plants is available to first-order consumers (herbivores). Of the remaining 90 percent of the energy, about half is used for life functions and the rest is lost as heat during respiration. Similarly, only about 10 percent of the food energy that makes up the body of an herbivore is available to the next level, the carnivore, and about 10 percent of the food energy of the carnivore is passed on to the omnivore. The exact percentage from one level to the next will vary with the organisms.

The general pattern showing the amount of food passed from producers to herbivores to carnivores and/or omnivores forms an energy pyramid, with the first level being the producers. Each level of an energy pyramid, as shown in this activity, from the producer to the top consumer (the top consumer in a food chain), has less available energy represented by the decreasing size of the layers.

BOUNCING

PURPOSE: To demonstrate how mechanical wave energy is transferred.

MATERIALS:

- box with one side at least 10 inches (25 cm) long
- 20 to 30 grains of rice
- pencil

PROCEDURE:

1. Set the box on a table.

2. Spread the grains of rice in a row across the top of the box.

3. With the eraser end of the pencil, gently tap on the top of the box near one end of the row of rice grains. Observe the movement of the rice grains.

4. Repeat step 3, but tap harder.

RESULTS When the box is tapped gently, all or most of the rice grains slowly bounce around, staying in about the same position on the box. Harder tapping causes the rice grains to quickly bounce around. Some lift off the box, moving to different places. The grains all appear to move at the same time, and the ones near the pencil move more.

WHY? Each tap pushes the box down when the pencil hits. Thus work is done on the box and energy is transferred to it. The repeated tapping disturbs the surface of the box, sending a mechanical wave across the surfaces of the box. The direction of the medium (box) disturbance is vertical (up and down) and the motion of the wave is horizontal (across the box). The wave moves so quickly that the rice grains appear to move at the same time. The grains near where the pencil taps move more because as a wave moves away from the source producing it, energy of the wave is lost.

Some of the energy is transferred to the grains of rice, some to air above the box, and some to the box itself. The grains bounce up and down but generally stay in the same position because the wave moving across the box carries energy, not material. So the grains are just temporarily disturbed from their original resting position but return to the approximate resting position when the wave passes. If the grains receive enough energy to be lifted above the box's surface, they may fall in a new location. This is because when the pencil is tapped hard against the box, it gives the wave more energy to transfer to the rice.

GLOSSARY

absorb To take in.

amplitude In reference to a wave, the maximum movement of the particles of a medium from their resting position.

antinodes The crests and troughs of a standing wave.

atom The building block of matter; the smallest part of an element that has all the properties of that element.

attraction The quality of pulling together.

autotroph An organism that can make its own food.

bond The force holding atoms together.

charge The property of particles within atoms that causes a force between the particles; also called electric charge.

frequency In reference to waves, the number of waves per unit of time.

friction The force that opposes the motion of two surfaces in contact with each other; a method of producing static electricity.

gravity The force that exists between objects due to their mass.

heat The energy that flows from a warm material to a cool material due to differences in temperature; energy transferred by conduction, convection, or radiation.

incandescent lamp A lamp whose lightbulb produces light by heating a filament to a high temperature.

inertia The tendency of an object in motion to continue to move forward.

infrared radiation Invisible radiation that is felt as heat, and its wave size is greater than red light; heat waves.

machine A device that helps a person do work.

mass The amount of material in a substance, measured in grams.

molecule The smallest physical unit of a compound.

photon A packet of energy that has both wave and particle properties.

pigment A natural substance that gives color to a material.

polarized A condition in which the positive and negative charges in a material are separated so that it has a positive and a negative end.

porous Having holes.

potential energy The stored energy of an object due to its position or condition.

radiation Energy traveling in the form of electromagnetic waves; the method in which heat is transferred in the form of electromagnetic waves; the emission of infrared radiation.

reflect To bounce back from a surface.

ultraviolet radiation (UV) Invisible radiation that can burn the skin; its wave size is smaller than violet light.

velocity Speed in a particular direction.

vibration Any motion that repeatedly follows the same path, such as a side-to-side or to-and-fro motion.

weight A measure of the force of gravity on an object.

white light A mixture of all the possible visible light waves.

work (w) The movement of an object by a force; the product of the force by the distance along which the force is applied. The process of transferring energy.

FOR MORE INFORMATION

American Institute of Physics (AIP)
One Physics Ellipse
College Park, MD 20740-3843
(301) 209-3100
Web site: http://www.aip.org
The AIP is a not-for-profit organization whose job is to promote knowledge in the science of physics.

Canadian Association of Physicists (CAP)
Suite 112, MacDonald Building
University of Ottawa
150 Louis Pasteur Priv.
Ottawa, ON K1N 6N5
Canada
(613) 562-5614
Web site: http://www.cap.ca
The CAP was founded in 1945 and serves to highlight achievements in Canadian physics and to pursue scientific, educational, and public policy.

Institute of Physics (IOP)
76 Portland Place
London W1B 1NT
England
+44 (0)20 7470 4800
Web site: http://www.iop.org
The IOP is a London-based organization that brings physicists together for collaboration and learning.

NASA
Public Communications Office
Suite 5K39
Washington, DC 20546-0001
(202) 358-0001
Web site: http://www.nasa.gov
NASA, or the National Aeronautics and Space
Administration, is the agency of the U.S. government
committed to space exploration and study.

The Science Club
4921 Preston/Fall-City Road
Fall City, WA 98024
(425) 222-5066
Web site: http://www.scienceclub.org
The Science Club was founded in 1987 and offers science
experiments to over one million elementary schoolchildren,
teachers, and parents through school assemblies, parent
and teacher workshops, television, video, and print.

Web Sites

Due to the changing nature of Internet links, Rosen Publishing
has developed an online list of Web sites related to the subject
of this book. This site is updated regularly. Please use this link to
access the list:

http://www.rosenlinks.com/scif/ener

FOR FURTHER READING

Bailey, R. A., and Don Rittner. *Encyclopedia of Chemistry.* New York, NY. Facts On File, 2005.

Ball, Jacqueline A., and Paul Barnett, et al. *Conservation and Natural Resources.* Chicago, IL: Gareth Stevens Publishing, 2004.

Bauman, Amy. *Earth's Natural Resources.* Strongsville, OH: Gareth Stevens Publishing, 2008.

Bortz, Fred. *The Electron.* New York, NY: Rosen Publishing, 2004.

Claybourne, Anna. *Forms of Energy.* Chicago, IL: Raintree, 2010.

Ford, Kenneth William. *The Quantum World: Quantum Physics for Everyone.* Cambridge, MA: Harvard University Press, 2004.

Galiano, Dean. *Electric and Magnetic Phenomena.* New York, NY: Rosen Publishing, 2011.

Gardner, Ralph. *Light, Sound and Waves Science Fair Projects: Using Sunglasses, Guitars, CDs and Other Stuff.* Berkeley Heights, NJ: Enslow Publishers, 2004.

Johanson, Paula. *Biofuels: Sustainable Energy in the 21st Century.* New York, NY: Rosen Publishing, 2010.

L'Annunziata, Michael F. *Radioactivity: Introduction and History.* Amsterdam, the Netherlands: Elsevier, 2007.

Malley, Marjorie Caroline. *Radioactivity: A History of a Mysterious Science.* New York, NY: Oxford, 2011.

Manning, Phillip. *Atoms, Molecules, and Compounds.* New York, NY. Chelsea House Publishers, 2008.

Orr, Tamra. *Motion and Forces*. New York, NY: Rosen Publishing, 2011.

Oxlade, Chris, Kirsteen Rogers, Corinne Stockley, and Jane Wertheim. *The Usborne Illustrated Dictionary of Chemistry*. Rev. ed. London, England: Usborne Children's Books, 2006.

Parker, Steve. *Making Waves: Sound*. Chicago, IL: Heinemann Library, 2005.

Smil, Vaclav. *Energy: A Beginner's Guide*. Oxford, England: Oneworld, 2006.

Solway, Andrew. *Exploring Forces and Motion*. New York, NY: Rosen Publishing, 2007.

Solway, Andrew. *Renewable Energy Sources*. Chicago, IL: Raintree, 2010.

Spilsbury, Louise. *A Sustainable Future: Saving and Recycling Resources*. Chicago, IL: Heinemann-Raintree, 2006.

Walker, Niki. *Biomass: Fueling Change*. New York, NY: Crabtree Publishing Company, 2007.

Weir, Jane. *Forces and Motion*. Mankato, MN: Compass Point Books, 2009.

Whiting, Jim. *The Science of Hitting a Home Run: Forces and Motion in Action*. Mankato, MN: Capstone Press, 2010.

Wolny, Philip. *Chemical Reactions*. New York, NY: Rosen Publishing, 2011.

INDEX

ABOUT THE AUTHOR

Janice VanCleave is a former award-winning science teacher who now spends her time writing and giving hands-on science workshops. She is the author of more than forty children's science books.

Designer: Nicole Russo; Editor: Nicholas Croce

All photos by Cindy Reiman, assisted by Karen Huang.